ARTHI

LAND AND LEGEND
by Kent Goodman

The real Arthur was never a king in any national sense, and certainly not of the English. In fact, the Anglo-Saxons who overran Britain in the late fifth century were his mortal enemies. Although he could never truly be called King Arthur, he did have a royal title. The monk Nennius, writing in the year 830, told of Arthur fighting *cum regibus Brittonum sed ipse dux erat bellorum* or, in other words, 'with the kings of the Britons, although he was the leader in battle'. With the kings? Not a king himself but a war leader? We just do not know. It may be the case, it may not. He was probably from a royal family of mixed Roman/Briton blood. The chronological clues to the existence of Arthur cover a hundred years or more, an impossible stretch of time for one person. They can't all be accommodated. While there may be an 'original' Arthur-figure somewhere in the time-range, stories about other men, perhaps other Arthurs, have got attached to him. He is a composite.

Although Arthur became famous across the whole of Britain (and around the world), most of his (true) exploits took place in the Wessex area. This was his home and it was well suited for someone of his stature – wild, romantic, spiritual, independent.

In the twelfth-century Geoffrey of Monmouth was the first person to popularize the idea of King Arthur as we know him today. Even though much of what he wrote was thought to be far-fetched, there was a basis of historical truth in it. He argued that he gained his knowledge by translating old books from the original Briton language and from the stories people told and remembered. His Arthur lived in a medieval kingdom, with knights in shining armour and ladies-in-waiting, grand feasts, magnificent castles, tournaments and all the other aspects of that society. The work became very popular and soon a torrent of stories about Arthur appeared. A French writer, Chrétien de Troyes, added most of the rest of the modern tale – the story of Guinevere and Launcelot and of the quest for the Holy Grail. He also borrowed heavily from Celtic myths and tradition, so in essence his stories, although made contemporary, had very early beginnings.

By AD410 the Romans had to abandon Britain to defend their positions in Europe. After they left, the Britons faced many invasions from neighbours anxious to get a piece of land for themselves. The Venerable Bede wrote in *c.* 731 that *in the year of our Lord 449 . . . the Angles and Saxons came to Britain at the invitation of King Vortigern . . . on condition that they protected the country; nevertheless their real intention was to attack it.* Later came warriors from *the three most formidable races of Germany, the Saxons, Angles and Jutes.*

PRESCELLY HILLS
The only area in Wales where the bluestones, the smaller stones in the centre of Stonehenge, could have come from. According to legend, Merlin magically transported them. They may have already been known for their healing properties.

**Arthur is said to have been born at
Tintagel 1500 years ago, as a result of magic and subterfuge.**

ARTHUR MAY LIE
SLEEPING, BUT HIS
SPIRIT IT STILL HERE
IN THE WIND THAT
WHISTLES ACROSS
THE CHALK DOWNS,
IN THE SOLITUDE OF
SALISBURY PLAIN, IN
THE CRASHING WAVES,
IN THE ANCIENT
SMALL HAMLETS, IN
THE STANDING
STONES, IN THE VERY
AIR YOU BREATHE.

Geoffrey of Monmouth was the first to suggest that Arthur was born at Tintagel, probably to please Reginald, the brother of Robert, his patron; the date of the birth is unclear. There may have been a Celtic monastery on the Cornish plateau and a medieval castle may well have been built here because of the glamour conferred on it by Geoffrey. It was thought that the legends of Arthur's connection with the fortress were just that – legend. However, recent digs have shown that the area was fortified probably during the middle fifth century, in Arthur's lifetime, and to further strengthen claims of Tintagel's authenticity a remarkable discovery was recently made.

A fourteen by eight inch (20 cm x 5 cm) piece of slate was found that was originally a plaque. It had not been disturbed since the sixth century, and it bore the inscription Pater Coliavificit Artognou – Artognou, father of Coll, had this building made. Since Artognou would have been pronounced Arthnou, this makes the inscription close enough to Arthur. In modern terms this would equate to an 'Arthur slept here' sign, in about 600, thus lending credibility to the Arthur story of Geoffrey's account, written 500 years later. Whatever was there, Tintagel undoubtedly had an important establishment and was, perhaps, a regional centre of government.

According to legend, Uther Pendragon, by now King of the Britons, held a great feast at Easter which all of his barons were expected to attend. The Duke of Cornwall, called Gorlois, was there with his beautiful wife, Ygerna. As soon as Uther set eyes on her he was smitten, so her husband took her away to the safety of the impregnable castle at Tintagel.

TINTAGEL

Tintagel, situated on a headland on the north coast of Cornwall and cut off from the mainland except for a narrow isthmus, is a wild and lonely place, swept by crashing waves. It looks dramatic enough to spawn legends.

Ygerna
Ygraine
Igraine
Eigyr

Ector
Hector

Then Uther sent for Merlin, that wise and subtle man with strange and secret powers of prophecy and those deceptions of the ordinary and the obvious which are called magic.

When they met, Merlin said brusquely,

"Sir, I know every corner of your heart and mind. And if you will swear by your anointed kingship to grant me my wish, you shall have what I know your heart desires."

And so great was Uther's eagerness that he swore by the four Evangelists to keep his promise.

Then Merlin said, "Sir, this is my desire. The first time you make love to Igraine she will conceive a child by you. When that child is born it must be given to me to do with as I wish. But I do promise that this will be to your honour and to the child's advantage. Do you agree?"

"It shall be as you wish," said the king.

"Then rise and make yourself ready." Merlin said. "This very night you will lie with Igraine in the castle of Tintagel by the sea."

[In due course] the child was delivered to Merlin, who carried it to Sir Ector, and his wife nursed the baby at her own breast. Then Merlin brought a holy man to christen the child and it was named Arthur.

DUNSTER
It was thought that Arthur spent his youth learning martial arts in either Celliwic, near Padstow in Cornwall, or Dunster in Somerset. If it were the latter, he would have been educated in the martial arts by Prince Cadwy. Arthur was crowned king at Silchester in Hampshire when he was fifteen.

CARMARTHEN
Merlin's birthplace according to Geoffrey of Monmouth.

Background:
Dunster Castle.

Tintagel

MERLIN

Merlin was already legendary in Welsh accounts. He was certainly a Welsh druid and famous bard, and was first mentioned in print by Geoffrey (although he probably got his name from Nennius, a ninth-century writer who mentioned Merddyn Wyllt, or 'the Wild'). He mentions the account of Vortigern's fortress, which kept falling down every time it was built. The king's seers tell him that it will keep happening unless the blood of a fatherless child is spilled on the foundations. After a search, Merlin is found, whose mother is a princess but whose father nobody knows (or, in other accounts, is the Devil).

Instead of being sacrificed, Merlin prophesizes that two dragons, one red (British) and the other white (Saxon) are fighting in a pool beneath the fortress. When the area is excavated, that is what is found. In a recent dig at Dinas Emrys, thought to have been where Vortigern's stronghold was situated, a pool or pond-like area was discovered beneath the rubble of an ancient fortification.

Merlin spends a good many years living as a hermit in the woods, having been driven mad by the carnage at the battle of Arderydd. His attributes suggest that the real Myrddyn is mixed up with various ancient Celtic deities; shaman (priests) would predict and enact their own death, as Merlin later did.

Merlin
Myrddyn

In the small cove resting at the bottom of Tintagel is a large cave, filled with the sea at regular intervals, although easy enough to explore at low tide. This is called Merlin's Cave and legend has it that the cave is haunted by Merlin's ghost.

Morgan-le-Fay is the evil one of Arthur's three half-sisters.
She sends Morgause to seduce him. Mordred is born.

S ome time after Arthur had become King by pulling the sword from the
stone (p.10) on which was written *Whoever pulls this sword from this stone
and anvil is King of all England by right of birth,* he
went with his followers to the city of Caerleon. Then to his court
came the wife of King Lot of Orkney who was a
very fair lady and Arthur desired her and made love to her and she
conceived a child by him who was to be Sir Mordred. The lady
remained a month in Arthur's court and then departed homeward.
And Arthur did not know that she was his half-sister and that,
unwitting, he had fallen into sin.
And his brooding fell on him again. He called Merlin and

questioned him. "Is the child you spoke of born?"
"Yes, my lord . . . on May Day" . . .
Then a cruel and cowardly plan grew in his mind with which to save
his honour and his life. He was ashamed to tell his plan to Merlin
before he put it into action. To conceal his incestuous sin, couriers
went out to all his barons and his knights, ordering that any male
child born on May Day must be sent to the king on pain of death . . .

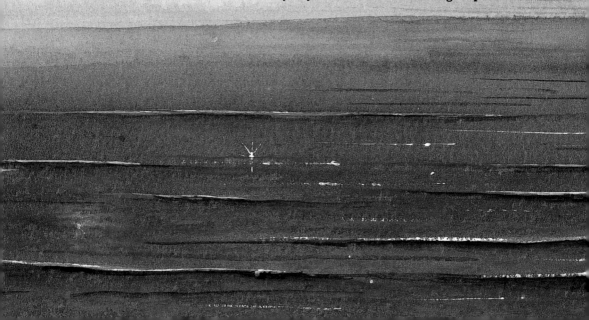

The baby Mordred escapes death and will later become
Arthur's Judas.

Then the king conveyed the babies to the coast, for he could
not bring himself to slaughter them. He placed the month-old
babies in a little ship and set the sail to an offshore wind
and it moved out to sea unattended. King Arthur, with
shamed and evil eyes, watched the little ship carry its
evidence of his fate away, shrinking in the distance. And
the king turned and rode heavily away.
The wind arose, shouting, and veered about and drove
the ship back on the land. Below a castle it struck a sunken
rock and spilled its wailing cargo into the waves.
On the shore a good man sitting in his hut heard a cry above
the whining wind and lash of surf. He walked to the beach
and in the soil he found a baby wedged in a bit of
wreckage. He took it up and warmed it under his cloak
and carried it home with him, and his wife took
Mordred to her breast and suckled him.

Mordred
Modred
Medrawt

Before Mordred was born Arthur had drawn the sword from the stone and become King of England.

When Arthur told Merlin that he loved Guinevere, the daughter of King Lodegrance of Camylarde, his friend replied,

Guinevere
Gwenhwyvar

"Well then, if I should tell you that Guinevere will be unfaithful to you with your dearest and most trusted friend – "
"I would not believe you." . . .

Lodegrance
Leodegrance

Then Lodegrance brought Guinevere to Merlin and also the Round Table, and a hundred knights richly armed and dressed.

In the Great Hall at Winchester Castle is King Arthur's Round Table, thought to have been made in the reign of Edward III (1344), who had wanted to establish a Knights of the Round Table order. However, one of the European kings beat him to it, so he founded the Order of the Garter instead. The table is, in fact, probably earlier and may have been made for Edward I who liked Arthurian entertainments. It was first painted in 1522 on the orders of Henry VIII. Its twenty-four segments are alternately green and white with the red Tudor rose in the middle. At the top is a portrait of King Arthur (which is actually a portrait of Henry VIII). Henry III built the Great Hall in 1232–40.

Each seat of the table had a knight's name written on it in gold letters, except two that Merlin said would be filled in due course. And so began the Knights of the Round Table.

The Round Table, Guinevere's dowry, provided the perfect
way to show that no knight was superior.

MOST FAMOUS KNIGHTS

Sir Kay (Cai)
As the son of Ector he was Arthur's foster-brother and became one of his doughty champions.

Sir Launcelot
He was raised by the Lady of the Lake and became Arthur's best friend and a brave fighter. His love for Guinevere destroyed the fellowship of the Round Table.

Sir Bedivere (Bedwyr)
One of Arthur's most prominent followers and a survivor of the last battle, when he was charged with flinging Excalibur into the lake.

Sir Bors
One of the three successful knights on the Grail Quest who, unlike the others, returned to Camelot and died later on crusade.

Sir Gawain (Gwalchmai, Gauvain, Gayain)
Son of Arthur's half-sister, Morgause, and a prominent knight.

Sir Galalad
Son of Sir Launcelot and Elaine, who died of love for her unfaithful husband, Galalad was the perfect knight and as such sat in the Siege Perilous. When he finally saw the Grail he expired from sheer bliss.

Sir Perceval (Peredur)
Son of Pellinore, Perceval's mother wanted him to know nothing of knighthood but he eventually became the hero of the Grail Quest.

The rules of the Round Table were simple:

Never to do outrage nor murder, and always to flee treason; also, by no means to be cruel, but to give mercy unto him that asketh mercy . . . and always to do ladies, damosels and gentlewomen succor, upon pain of death . . . and to take no battle in a wrongful quarrel for no law, nor for world's gain.

Arthur also made it a rule that nobody could eat until someone told a story of great derring-do. Fortunately, there was never a shortage of tales to tell, so unusual and so challenging were their adventures.

SIR HELIN · SIR GALAHAD · KING ARTHVR · SIR LAVNCELOT · SIR KAY

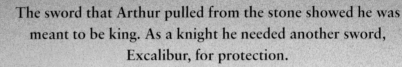

The sword that Arthur pulled from the stone showed he was meant to be king. As a knight he needed another sword, Excalibur, for protection.

Before he married, Arthur had drawn the sword, which was originally called Caliburn and had been forged in Avalon, out of a stone (a sarsen stone at Avebury or Stonehenge?).

"And how did you get this sword?" [asked Sir Ector].
Arthur said, "When I rode back for my brother's sword, I found no one at home, so I could not get it. I did not want my brother to be without a sword so I came here and took the sword from the stone for him."
"Were there no knights here guarding the sword?" Sir Ector asked.
"No, sir", said Arthur. "There was no one here."
Sir Ector was silent for a time and then he said, "I understand now that you must be king of this land." . . .

Some time passed and Arthur met a brave knight who, not knowing Arthur was the king, challenged him and deprived him of both spear and sword. Arthur was saved from death by Merlin who cast a sleeping spell on the knight (who was King Pellinore). Then Merlin took Arthur to a broad lake of clear water.

And in the middle of the lake Arthur saw an arm with a sleeve of rich white silk, and the hand held up a sword by its scabbard . . .
Merlin asked, "Which do you like better, the sword or the scabbard?"
"The sword, of course," said Arthur.
"The scabbard is far more precious," said Merlin. "While you wear the scabbard you can lose no blood no matter how deeply you are wounded. It is a magic scabbard. You will do well to keep it always near you."

Excalibur was given to Arthur by the Lady of the Lake which separates life from death. Beyond the Lake was Avalon.

Right:
The Damsel of the Holy Grail by Dante Gabriel Rossetti, a pre-Raphaelite painter who was particularly drawn to the yearning mysticism of the Grail legend. In the legend the Grail was carried by a pure virgin. Here she is crowned by the dove of the Holy Spirit.

The Grail Quest is the most important quest for the Knights of the Round Table.

The Grail, or at least a magical cup like it, is featured in religions of many different races, including Russian, Indian, Japanese and the Celts (the cauldron of Bran). Chrétien de Troyes was the first one we know of to write about it, in the late twelfth-century, in the tale of Perceval and the Grail.

In this story the bumbling Sir Perceval arrives at the Grail castle, having been told where it was by a man fishing from a boat – the Fisher King – who has an unhealing wound in his thigh. (In the original stories, based on Welsh and Celtic myth, the king was wounded in the genitals. This has strong associations with the pagan belief that the health of the king influenced the health of the land.) This caused the land around to be barren and was seen as a possible cause of the ills of the whole of Britain. To reverse this situation the Grail must be won by the raising of a special question: what is the Grail and whom does it serve? However, Sir Perceval has been told by his mother not to ask any questions, so he doesn't. The next day he awakes on a pile of rocks – the castle is gone.

In other versions, the knight is usually dumbfounded, before he has chance to speak, by the magical procession of a damsel carrying a dish, and another with a carving platter who is accompanied by a squire with a bleeding lance. If the knight has asked the question, all would have disappeared and the Fisher King would have been healed.

These stories have inspired great works of art, epic poetry and passionate music.

PAIMPONT, BRITTANY

The Centre de L'Imaginaire Arthurien now occupies the Chateau of Comper-en-Brocéliande (shown here), near Paimpont, Brittany. Tradition has it that Merlin created a castle for Nimue, the Lady of the Lake, in the nearby lake. Nimue was said to have brought up Launcelot here, teaching him to be the best of knights.

Nimue, the Lady of the Lake, entrances Merlin and brings about his disappearance.

Then Nyneve, with the inborn craft of maidens, began to question Merlin about his magic arts, half promising to trade her favours for his knowledge. And Merlin, with the inborn helplessness of men, even though he foresaw her purpose, could not forbear to teach her. And as they crossed back to England and rode slowly from the coast toward Cornwall, Merlin showed her many wonders and, when at last he found that he interested her, he showed her how the magic was accomplished and put in her hands the tools of enchantment, gave her the antidotes of magic against magic and, finally, in his aged folly, taught her those spells which cannot be broken by any means. And when she slapped her hands in maidenly joy, the old man, to please her, created a room of unbelievable wonders under a great rock cliff, and with his crafts he furnished it with comfort and richness and beauty to be the glorious apartment for the consummation of their love. And they two went through a passage in the rock to the room of wonders, hung with gold and lighted with many candles. Merlin stepped in to show it to her, but Nyneve leaped back and cast the awful spell that cannot be broken by any means, and the passage closed and Merlin was trapped inside for all time to come. She could hear his voice faintly through the rock, pleading for release. And Nyneve mounted her horse and rode away. And Merlin remains there to this day, as he knew he would.

MARLBOROUGH
There is a mound in the grounds of Marlborough College that is probably prehistoric, was pointed out as Merlin's grave, and is now known as Merlin's Mount. In 1215 this was said to be the derivation of the town's name.

Nyneve
Nimue
Niniane
Viviane
Viviene

MOUSEHOLE
'There shall land on the Rock of Merlin
Those who shall burn Paul, Penzance and Newlyn.'
Merlin's Rock rises from the water near the quay where the wizard delivered this prophecy which was fulfilled in 1595 by a Spanish flotilla.

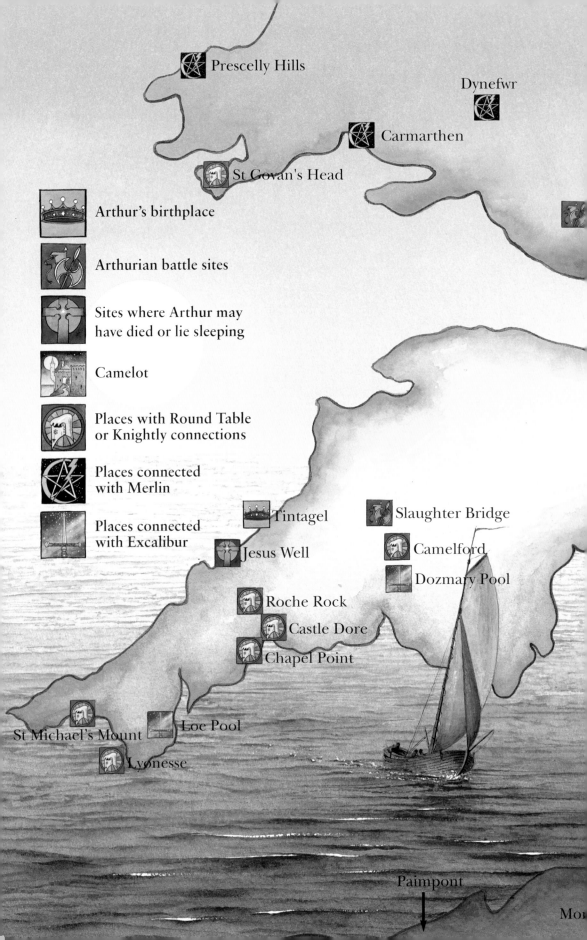

Prescelly Hills

Dynefwr

Carmarthen

St Govan's Head

Arthur's birthplace

Arthurian battle sites

Sites where Arthur may
have died or lie sleeping

Camelot

Places with Round Table
or Knightly connections

Places connected
with Merlin

Places connected
with Excalibur

Tintagel

Slaughter Bridge

Jesus Well

Camelford

Dozmary Pool

Roche Rock

Castle Dore

Chapel Point

St Michael's Mount

Loe Pool

Lyonesse

Paimpont

Mo

Brecon Beacons

Caerwent

Caerleon

Brent Knoll

Swindon

White Horse

Liddington Fort

Bath

Marlborough

Amesbury

Glastonbury

Salisbury Plain

Winchester

Old Sarum

Cadbury Castle

Badbury Rings

chel

WINCHESTER
Winchester was thought to be Camelot by Geoffrey of Monmouth. Sir Launcelot agrees to wear the favour of the Lady of Astolat (later, Shallot) at the Winchester jousts.

Camelot itself could either be Winchester in Hampshire, Caerwent or Caerleon in Wales, or Cadbury Castle in Somerset. Archaeological digs have confirmed a Neolithic and Iron Age settlement at Cadbury that was re-fortified in the fifth and sixth centuries. Excavations revealed that the outer banks of the fort were fortified with stone and timber walls, and there was a great hall in the centre of the complex, made of timber and probably thatch. Its very size meant it was clearly an important centre and a royal one as well, judging by the imported pottery found there.

The antiquarian John Leland, travelling in the area in 1542, identified the hillfort with "Camallate, sumtyme a famose toun or castelle". Although there was a town called Camel (now Queen Camel and West Camel) near the hillfort, any attempt to link it etymologically with the Camelot of fame is useless, because this name was given to Arthur's castle by the French author Chrétien de Troyes in the twelfth-century, much later than the ancient town of Camel. The Welsh Triads place Arthur's seat at either Callington or Killiberry in Cornwall.

Right:
This reconstruction painting of Tintagel in the fifth century shows what a small fortification on the coast may have been like. The drawings opposite are based on historical evidence of the construction of a gatehouse and ramparts at what was thought to be Arthur's Camelot, Cadbury Castle.

The Round Table is at Camelot so the
knights return here after their adventures
(which are the subject of another book).

CAERLEON

Geoffrey of Momouth gives Caerleon as the site where Arthur, a mighty monarch, holds court after subduing all enemies in Britain and in his empire overseas. The town boasts the best amphitheatre in Britain, described by some as the Round Table. Caerleon is where Arthur fought his ninth battle.

CAERWENT

William Caxton, who printed and published Malory's *Morte d'Arthur* in 1485 may have been referring to Caerwent when he spoke of the ruins of Camelot being visible in Wales.

CADBURY CASTLE

Glastonbury Tor and Brent Knoll are sometimes visible from this Iron Age fort that holds a greater claim to being Arthur's Cadbury than any other site. Archeology has found that it was a well used and important defence in Arthur's time . . . 'the people can tell nothing there but that they have heard Arthur much resorted to Camalat' (Leland, 1542).

Glastonbury, a place of magic and spirituality, is thought of as Avalon.

GLASTONBURY

Glastonbury in Somerset has always been a spiritual place for Britons, perhaps because Joseph of Arimathea is said to have established a Christian church here within living memory of Jesus. Saints, including Patrick, Columba and Bridget, are said to have lived here. Perhaps it was because of its pervasive sense of magic and spirituality that Arthur himself was thought to have been taken here when he died.

One of Britain's best travel writers, H. V. Morton, recorded the Grail story in 1927. 'For centuries men believed that in AD61 St. Philip sent Joseph of Arimathaea, whose hands had laid Christ in the tomb, to preach the Gospel in England. He is said, according to the later legend, to have come with a band of missionaries bearing the Chalice of the Last Supper, which he had begged of Pilate. This Chalice (the Grail) had held the Sacred Blood from the Cross. Here in this English meadow Joseph of Arimathaea is said to have built England's first church of plaited oziers.

When the missionaries crossed Weary-all Hill ('weary-all' with the journey), Joseph, so the famous old story goes, planted his staff in the earth. It took root and grew into the famous Glastonbury Thorn.'

During an expensive refurbishment of the Abbey in the 12th century the monks were fortunate enough to discover a tomb bearing the words *His lacet Arthurus, rex quondam, rexque futurus* — 'Here lies Arthur, the once and future king'.

The presence of the Grail is what is thought to give the water of Chalice Well, at the foot of Weary-all Hill, its red tint. The water is said to have healing properties, which is one indicator that suggests Glastonbury was once a powerful pagan site; healing waters, mysterious and magical cups or cauldrons, final resting places for kings and queens, are all strong pagan motifs.

The dolorous stroke received by Pelham (or the Fisher King) causes blight to spread over the land so that it becomes the wasteland.

This Glastonbury, this Avalon, has been the birthplace of 'two of the greatest epics that have come from the English mind: one is of the Holy Grail and the other of a wounded king' (H.V. MORTON). Malory expands: **"Not long after Jesus Christ was crucified,"** [Merlin said] **"Joseph, a merchant of Arimathea who gave our Lord his sepulcher, came sailing to this land bringing the sacred cup of the Last Supper filled with the holy blood and also that spear with which Longinus the Roman pierced the side of Jesus on the Cross. And Joseph brought these holy things to the Island of Glass in Avalon and there he built a church, the first in all this land. That was Joseph's body on the bed and that Longinus's spear, and with it you wounded Pelham, Joseph's descendant, and it was the dolorous stroke I spoke of long ago. And because you have done this, a blight of sickness and hunger and despair will spread over the land."**

After the search for the Grail is over most of Arthur's knights are dead or old and the younger Mordred comes to the fore. He knows that Launcelot and Guinevere are lovers and makes sure that he discovers them together. When he does, he forces Arthur to condemn his bride to death.

Reluctantly, Arthur agrees, but Launcelot saves her at the last minute. Arthur follows him, but while he is away Mordred claims that his father is dead and that he is now king, so Arthur hurries back to fight him. He corners Mordred in Richborough, but he escapes. He tries to do battle with him again at Winchester, but again Mordred is able to slip away.

Pelham
Pellinore
Parlen
Pellean
Pellehan
Pellam
(often the
Fisher King)

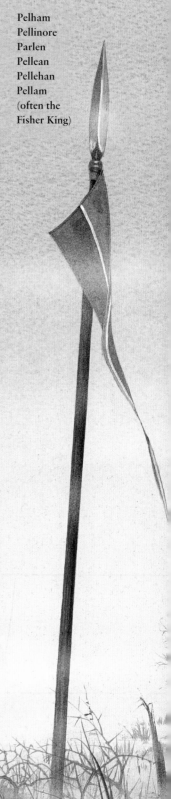

BATH

Why is Bath associated with Mount Badon? The early name for Bath was Caerfaddon in Welsh, *caer* meaning city and *faddon* meaning 'of Baddon'. According to near contemporary accounts, Arthur was said to have fought at mons Badonicus or at monte Badonis 'on the hill of Bado'. In the Welsh language, two ds together (dd) were (and are) pronounced 'th', so Baddon would have been pronounced 'Bathon', a close etymological link. In addition, the Britons would have been fighting the Saxons in just such an area, as compared to the Picts and Scots whom they fought further north.

Lansdown Hill, Bath. Could this be the site of the Battle of Badon?

According to some sources Ambrosius Aurelianus, the King of the Britons, in about 470 led a campaign against the Saxons at Badon Hill, most likely near Bath (on Lansdown Hill?), but the battle could also have taken place at Liddington Castle near Swindon, or even Baydon Hill or Badbury Rings. During the fighting the great leader was killed. It was then that the young Arthur, who was with him, took over and totally defeated the enemy, driving them back to their homes in the east (Saxony).

> Arthur, as a post-Roman battle leader, was the best
> of his kind and the most successful.

The battle was caused by treachery on the part of the Saxons. After being defeated in the north the invaders promised to return to their own country. However, they simply circled their ships around and landed at Torbay, from where they fought their way to Bath, pillaging as they went. Arthur, furious at the deception, raced south to meet them and besieged them for three days. Presumably, he didn't want to attack them at once since they held the top of the hill, the most advantageous position. By the third day, the Britons seemed to be losing ground.

Arthur, wearing his usual leather jerkin and gold helmet emblazoned with a dragon, charged up the hill by himself. He carried a shield called Pridwen that had the likeness of the Virgin Mary on it. He was armed with the famous sword Caliburn (Excalibur), along with a spear called Ron, which was 'long, broad in the blade and thirsty for slaughter'. As he advanced up the hill he cut down between 470 and 960 men (accounts vary). Not surprisingly, his own men were greatly encouraged by this and joined in the charge, routing the enemy completely.

The significance of this battle was its complete destruction of the enemy. Until the battle of Badon, the Britons were sometimes the winners, sometimes the losers, in a seemingly never-ending series of engagements. However, this was such a crushing blow that peace was finally restored (to the Wessex area of England, at least) for almost fifty years. In fact, history shows that many Saxons did indeed start to migrate back to their own countries around this time.

BADBURY RINGS
Another possible location for the Battle of Mount Badon, although the early pronunciation of Badbury would have meant something like 'Badda's fort', a Saxon name, and it is not thought likely that a victorious British army would have given the site the enemy's name.

ARTHUR'S TWELVE VICTORIES

1. Glein
2. Dubglas
3. Dubglas
4. Dubglas
5. Dubglas
6. Bassus
7. In the wood of Celidon (Caledonia)
8. By Castle Guinnion
9. In the City of the Legion (Chester? Caerleon?)
10. On the bank of the river Tribuit
11. On the hill called Agned
12. On Mount Badon

Mordred tells Arthur that Guinevere and Launcelot are together. Launcelot rescues Guinevere from being burned at the stake. She returns to Arthur . . .

CAMELFORD
Finally, Arthur catches up with Mordred here at Slaughter Bridge, over the River Camel.

CHARFORD
There could be some historical reasons to suppose that the battle of Camlann actually occurred at Charford, a few miles south of Salisbury. This is the site of a battle dated to 519, called the battle of Certicesford (the old name for Charford). This was the last battle fought by the Saxon Cerdic, after whom the area is named. If Mordred had sided with the Saxons to usurp King Arthur's territory (as Geoffrey states), a battle between a Cerdic/Mordred alliance and Arthur's army here is the most likely explanation, as well as being the only battle whose date is recorded.

SLAUGHTER BRIDGE
Supposedly the site of Camlann. The stone that commemorates the battle has an inscription that reads *Latini hic iacit filius Magiri* 'Latinus. Here he lies, son of Magarus'. Archaeological finds show that this is much more likely to commemorate a later Saxon battle of 825.

Malory sites the battle of Camlann on Salisbury Plain, following the example in the Vulgate Cycle (first started *c.* 1210). On the battlefield, Arthur tells his knight to throw Excalibur in 'yonder waterside'. If we accept that the battle took place on Salisbury Plain, the waterside must have been situated there. The Wylie, the Avon, the Bourne and the Nadder all cross the Plain. If you take the waterside to mean a large body of water, then the confluence of the Avon, Bourne and Nadder, now within the city of Salisbury, seems a strong possibility.

After the battle, which was held in mists so thick no-one could be sure if they were fighting friend or foe, only three people were left alive – Mordred, Arthur and Sir Bedivere. Arthur and Mordred fought each other, Mordred dying and Arthur left with a fatal head injury.

According to Geoffrey of Monmouth, when Arthur was mortally wounded he handed over the crown of Britain to his cousin Constantine, son of Cador, Duke of Cornwall, in the year 542.

While the actual story of Arthur and Mordred may be partly imaginary, a battle between two British armies probably happened in Arthur's real life. After the Saxons were pacified, the inter-tribal feuding began again and civil war must have broken out, with one of Arthur's kinsmen as his rival.

The battle of Camlann is also mentioned as taking place in 537, when Arthur and Medraut fell and there was plague in England and Ireland. Unfortunately, almost none of the battles can be positively identified. The battle in the Caledonian wood must have taken place in Scotland, but all the rest are debatable.

Arthur used his Roman heritage to his advantage and fought in the Roman way, that is, on horseback. This enabled him and his band of warriors to strike deep into enemy territory one week and fight again in another remote part of the kingdom the next. This mobility amazed and astounded not only his foes but also the general populace, and it wasn't long before truly amazing feats were attributed to him.

and Arthur goes to France to fight Launcelot. Mordred takes the kingdom. Arthur returns, fights, loses his scabbard and receives a mortal blow. Sir Bedivere throws his sword into water.

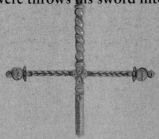

After the battle of Camlann, Arthur ordered Excalibur to be thrown into a lake.

There is evidence that the swords of leading warriors were sometimes sunk in pools when they died; the points were bent, or they were weighed down with stones, so that no-one else could use them – the sword was personal to its owner.

The story also has definite Celtic overtones, because people used to throw precious objects into holy pools, especially to appease a water goddess – in this case, the Lady of the Lake. We still make offerings to water deities today when we throw pennies into wells.

The sword in the stone could have pagan overtones as well. According to ancient custom, when two rivals within a tribe had a quarrel they would duel, not always to the death. As a sign that the loser would accept the decision, the winner would be given a special sword that had lain upon a sacred stone throughout the contest.

DOZMARY POOL
Last resting place of Excalibur. Malory writes how Sir Bedivere takes the sword from Arthur. 'Take thou Excalibur, my good sword, and go with it to yonder water side, and when thou comest there I charge thee throw my sword in that water, and come again and tell what thou seest.'

Bedivere tries to throw it away twice but balks and sees nothing. On the third time he throws it the Lady of the Lake grabs it, brandishes it three times and disappears below the surface. The actual Excalibur connection is probably a fairly recent fancy in the aftermath of Tennyson.

LOE POOL
Another contender for the place where Excalibur was thrown.

CORNWALL

BODMIN
A fight broke out in a church here in 1113 between Frenchmen and Cornishmen over the existence of Arthur. Arthur's Chair, Oven, Bed and Hall still retain links with this tradition.

BODMIN MOOR, site of Arthur's Bed, Chair, Hall and Oven.

CAMELFORD, page 22.

CASTLE-AN-DINAS
A fine hill-fort where Duke Gorlois was reputed to have died fighting Uther. Also known as Arthur's Hunting Lodge.

CASTLE DORE, B3269 near Fowey
King Mark, Iseult's husband in the Tristan romance, has strong links here which are fully explored in another book in this series.

DOZMARY POOL, Bodmin Moor, page 23.

FOWEY
The Tristan Stone commemorates the story of one of Arthur's principal knights.

KELLIWIC (Castle Killibury or Kelly Rounds, near Wadebridge)
A Cornish stronghold where Arthur lived and held court (in Welsh tradition).

Loe Pool, page 23.

MARAZION
From here the causeway runs out to St Michael's Mount which has connections with Arthur through a raven, an 18th-century sportsman and an old gentleman who thought the bird might be of royal blood (King Arthur himself, perhaps).

MOUSEHOLE, page 13.

PENDEEN, north of St Just
Arthur is said to have vanquished giants here with his cross-sword.

ST COLUMB MAJOR
There is a stone here with four hoofprints of Arthur's horse imprinted on it.

ST DENNIS
A possible site for Uther's siege of Dimilioc and death of Duke Gorlois.

ST LEVAN, near Porthcurno
Arthur is said to have made a journey here with Merlin who prophesied the end of the world.

SCILLY ISLES
Great Arthur and Little Arthur are two of these tiny islands which share in the formation of the Legend of Lyonesse.

SLAUGHTER BRIDGE, page 22.

TINTAGEL, page 3.

TREGEARE ROUNDS
The Dimilioc of Geoffrey of Monmouth.

TREREEN DINAS
Arthur's 'castle' in the Zennor legend.

ZENNOR, between Land's End and St Ives
The legend here concerns Arthur, Cornish kings and some menacing red-headed Danes.

DEVON

LUNDY ISLAND
A place from which the mysterious realm of Annwn can be entered.

DORSET
BADBURY RINGS, page 20.

HAMPSHIRE

PORTCHESTER
This may be Llongborth.

WINCHESTER, page 16.

HEREFORD & WORCESTER

ARTHUR'S CAVE, NE of Monmouth.
Perhaps a hiding place for troops.

ARTHUR'S STONE, near Dorstone.
A prehistoric grave mound that was later connected with Arthur.

SOMERSET

ARTHUR'S BRIDGE, A371 over the river Alham, Somerset.
BATH, page 20.

BRENT KNOLL
A link in the chain of hills that bear witness to the 'Arthurian beacon' theory. Cadbury Castle, Glastonbury Tor, Brent Knoll and Dinas Powys are visually linked in a straightish line.

CADBURY CASTLE, page 17.

RIVER CAM, crossed by the A303 east of Sparkford. A candidate for Camlann.

CARHAMPTON, between Minehead and Watchet
A legend concerning Arthur, a monk, an altar and a serpent was written in an early saint's 'Life'.

DUNSTER, page 4.

GLASTONBURY, page 18.

LANGPORT
Sometimes said to be the battle site of Llongborth. Above the altar of the parish church are stained-glass windows, one of which shows Joseph of Arimathaea.

SOUTH WALES
CAERLEON, page 17.

CAERWENT, page 17.

CARMARTHEN, page 4.

ST GOVAN'S HEAD and CHAPEL
The site of Sir Gawain's retirement after Arthur's passing and subsequent burial?

DINAS POWYS
A link in the 'Arthurian-beacon' chain that has traces of a fifth-century chieftain's home.

LLANCARFAN, north-west of Barry
A monastery was founded here and Arthurian traditions are drawn upon in several 'Lives' of Welsh saints written by monks.

LLANTWIT MAJOR, between Bridgend and Barry
This was originally a monastic community, founded by Saint Illtud who is said to have been a cousin of Arthur. A church dedicated to him on Caldey Island provides more clues to the connection.

CRAIG-Y-DINAS, the head of the Vale of Neath.
An elaborate version of the cave-legend, concerning a stranger, sleeping knights and avarice, takes place here.

ARTHUR'S STONE, near Reynoldston
Concerns a legend in which Arthur himself is a giant.

WILTSHIRE
AMESBURY. The site of an early monastery, founded possibly by Arthur's uncle or later by the Saxon queen Elfrida. Malory claims that Guinevere, after the passing of Arthur, retires to Amesbury Abbey (a convent) and says farewell to Launcelot here.

CHARFORD, south of Salisbury, near Breamore, page 22.

Liddington Castle, A345 near the M4. A possible candidate for Badon.

MARLBOROUGH, page 13.

SALISBURY PLAIN, page ii.
Geoffrey of Monmouth associates Stonehenge with Merlin and later Camlann is thought to have been sited on the Plain and it was here that Arthur received his mortal wound.

STONEHENGE, page 1.

FRANCE
PAIMPONT, Brittany, page 13.

LYONESSE - One of several legendary submerged lands, this one is off the southernmost point of Cornwall, in Mount's Bay.

LLONGBORTH - The scene of a battle in a Welsh elegy, mentioning Arthur. The name probably means 'warship port' and may well be Portchester in Hampshire.

DIMILIOC is where Geoffrey of Monmouth sites the death of Gorlois, Duke of Cornwall. He probably means the prehistoric camp of Tregeare Rounds, close to Tintagel.

CAMELOT, page 16.

CAMLANN, page 22.

MOUNT BADON, page 20.

AVALON a Celtic Otherworld, a mysterious and magic realm older than Christianity but with links to it through the Grail.

ANNWN a Celtic Otherworld which features in Welsh legend. Glastonbury Tor and Lundy Island are two of its points of access.

ASTOLAT which is later known as Shallot.

The importance of Arthur seemed to diminish in men's minds after his glorious medieval period, although he was still strong enough in the minds of kings for Henry VII to name his first son Arthur. Unfortunately, the lad died young and his brother Henry (VIII) succeeded their father. Four centuries later William Blake, that visionary and difficult poet-prophet whose 'Jerusalem' is the only one of his poems known by most people today, saw Arthur as a symbol of humanity: 'The giant Albion was Patriarch of the Atlantic, he is the Atlas of the Greeks . . . the stories of Arthur are the Acts of Albion, applied to a prince of the fifth-century who conquered Europe and held the empire of the world in the dark ages.' This must be the 'most unexpected and rapid reincarnation the Hero of the Britons ever experienced' (Gwyn Williams).

Malory's *Morte d'Arthur* underwent a revival and had a great influence on Tennyson, who later became Poet Laureate. Tennyson's *Idylls of the King*, published 1859–75, the Arthurian frescoes in the Royal Robing Room of the House of Lords and the beautiful, artistic, romantic paintings of the Pre-Raphaelite brotherhood, inspired by tales of the Knights of the Round Table, gave Arthur a firm place in the public consciousness once more. 'A nation receptive to royalism again was presented just at the right moment, with its Laureate's unfolded daydream of Christian monarchy firmly linked to the queen [Victoria] and her almost canonised husband [Albert]' (Geoffrey Ashe). For a fuller treatment of the resurrection of Arthur see Gwyn Williams, *Excalibur*.

Right:
The bodies Arthur and Guinevere being moved by Glastonbury monks around 1143 to be reburied.

Below:
This Plaque shows the place where Arthur and Guinevere were re-interred at Glastonbury.

SITE OF KING ARTHUR'S TOMB.
IN THE YEAR 1191 THE BODIES OF
KING ARTHUR AND HIS QUEEN WERE
SAID TO HAVE BEEN FOUND ON THE
SOUTH SIDE OF THE LADY CHAPEL.
ON 19TH APRIL 1278 THEIR REMAINS WERE
REMOVED IN THE PRESENCE OF
KING EDWARD I AND QUEEN ELEANOR
TO A BLACK MARBLE TOMB ON THIS SITE.
THIS TOMB SURVIVED UNTIL THE
DISSOLUTION OF THE ABBEY IN 1539

A rthur is an enigma: although we think of him in his medieval costume – suited in gleaming armour, with blond beard and blond hair streaming out from a dazzling jewelled crown – we also know that the real man was something else. And yet, even though the real Arthur was probably short, dark and swarthy, wearing a leather jerkin and cap, he is no less heroic, because the true matter of Arthur, as in people in general, is not so much what he looks like, but what he stands for.

Arthur bravely stands for everything that we wish we had the courage to. He fights the oppressors even against tremendous odds; he takes jealous pride in his own country; he protects and honours all women; he is loyal to his friends even when they do not return the favour; he believes in himself and his Just Cause.

Arthur is said to be sleeping with his men inside a cave, waiting for the right moment to return in Britain's hour of need. But with the extraordinary interest in Arthur at the moment, and the sense of pride and history that goes with it, perhaps his spirit has already started to return.

Cast your eyes at the landscape around you, at the soft rolling hills and clear streams, the bountiful farmlands, fields dotted with sheep and churches. Breathe in the sense of timelessness. This is the country that meant so much to Arthur and his men that they laid down their lives to protect it.

This is Arthur's land.